EASY OBJECT STORIES

LUTHER S. CROSS

BAKER BOOK HOUSE
Grand Rapids, Michigan 49506

Copyright 1984
by Baker Book House Company

ISBN: 0-8010-2502-8

Fifth printing, July 1990

Printed in the United States of America

Contents

Instructions

I have included a section on making and using puppets near the end of this volume, but in order to present more new material I have omitted the information on children's sermon techniques found in my other books. For more help in presenting story sermons, object lessons, picture and chalk talks, and puppet shows, see my books *Story Sermons for Children* (Grand Rapids: Baker Book House, 1966) or *Object Lessons for Children* (Baker Book House, 1967). These books describe making *glove puppets*.

When alternative methods are given, pick the handiest one.

Increase interest by varying the medium used: pictures are powerful, kids love puppets and the fun objects are just that. If you're afraid to draw before an audience, get a church member to make giant predrawn pictures. This book shows extremely easy ways to make puppets.

Important: The visuals often call for you to stick things to something, including to your body. If you make loops out of masking tape, sticky side out, they can be put out of sight between the objects to be joined. Keep this in mind, as this technique isn't repeated with each reference to sticking.

1

Love Sees Beauty in Everyone

Love is kind.   (1 Cor. 13:4)

Can you imagine Connie Crocodile, Jenny Giraffe, and Ellie Elephant dressed in tiny fluffy skirts, doing a ballet? They looked like a leaping log, a goat on stilts, and a giant, waltzing watermelon. They kept falling over each other and yelling, "Hey, look at me! I'm so pretty." But they laughed at each other's big mouth, neck, or nose.

Does Jesus think anyone's shape or color is ugly?

After their dancing knocked down their house, Jenny Giraffe said, "With my lovely neck, I'm going to be Miss Universe."

"Ugh!" said the elephant. "That wrec'· of a neck under your little head looks like a seasick golf club. But my gorgeous elephant body could model bikini swimsuits."

"Ugh!" said the crocodile. "Your nose-like-a-hose takes a week to sneeze. But my cute little dimpled crocodile smile could model lipstick on TV."

"Ugh!" said the giraffe. "Those jaws-like-saws are so big that when you yawn, half your insides are on the outside."

They were just about to start a fist fight when they heard a baby hippopotamus crying. It sounded sad and scared.

"I lost my ma-ma-mommy," it said, sobbing as if its heart would break.

"Don't worry, darling," said the elephant. "We'll find her."

Connie, Jenny, and Ellie looked until they found the mother hippopotamus. Then the baby and mommy ran into each other's arms, smiling from ear to ear. Their love made them beautiful.

"I'm sorry I insulted both of you," said the crocodile to the giraffe and elephant. "I just realized that we may look different, but everyone is beautiful if you love them."

7

Easy Object Lesson

Stick a large wiggle eye on your hand and make the animals as shown in figure 1.

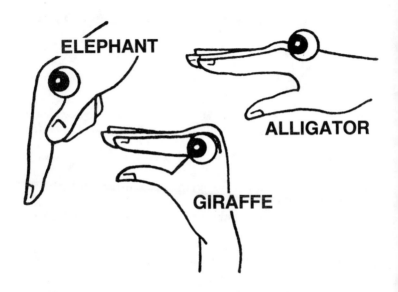

ELÉPHANT

ALLIGATOR

GIRAFFE

Figure 1   **Easy Object Lesson**

Fun Object Lesson

Giraffe: Before presenting the lesson, attach a paper horn, ear, and eye (2″ in diameter) on a man's shoe. Hold the shoe with your hand stuck up the leg of large pajama bottoms (see figure 2A). Open the pajama fly to give you more room. Animate the giraffe with jerky little shoe movements.

Elephant: Drop the shoe and fall to the position shown in figure 2B. Hold it long enough for people to wonder what you're doing. Then instantly create an elephant by sticking an eye on the pajama cloth over your temple. The oval paper

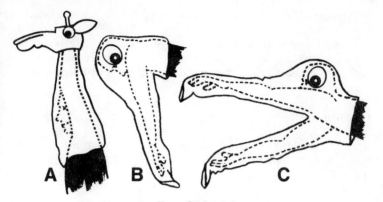

Figure 2 **Fun Object Lesson**

eye (3-1/2″ × 4″), should have a black pupil with a white highlight and a thick outline. Bugle like an elephant and curl the trunk over the back of your head then forward toward your chin.

Crocodile: Change into a crocodile by showing your other arm (figure 2C), which has been in the other pajama leg,

Figure 3 **Chalk Talk**

behind your body (when it wasn't applying the giraffe head or the elephant eye).

Using these instructions, begin your talk by showing the three animals whose neck, trunk, and mouth make them different. Then remove the pajama bottom and tell the story.

Puppet Talk

Hold a single glove puppet (see page 5) in the positions shown in figure 1. The elephant's trunk is a sock over the puppet's upper jaw.

Chalk Talk

See figure 3. Predraw part of the animals' bodies to save time.

2

Lonesome Candle

Where two or three come together in my name, there am I with them. (Matt. 18:20)

"I can be a Christian all by myself," Lonesome Candle told everyone. "Just don't bother me and I won't bother you." So she stayed alone in her comfortable closet. But she found out that it was hard to shine for Jesus all by herself. She couldn't see herself to know how lovely her light shone or to be inspired by it. And she kept falling over—Thud!—and losing her flame.

One day a sad voice called, "Lonesome Candle! Lonesome Candle!"

"Who are you?" she asked.

"I'm Jesus," said the voice. "How dare you hide Me in this closet!"

"How could I do that?" she said.

Jesus replied, "Your light could lead people to Me. When you hide it, you hide Me. Just look out of your door."

Lonesome Candle looked out and saw a world full of lost unlit candles wandering about and weeping. Then she heard a cry: "Help! Help! We're lost."

Following the cry out into an alley, she found two candles sobbing in a dark hole where they had fallen.

After Lonesome Candle pulled them out, they said, "Help us. We keep falling over and losing the flame of our enthusiasm. Join us so we can be a church. For Jesus is always present where two or three meet as Christians."

So Lonesome Candle joined hands with them as a church and they held each other up. Seeing each other's flames inspired each of them to burn brighter. When one of their flames died, the others lit it. When they weren't outside looking for lost candles, they burned in a window for all to see. So,

11

outside in the darkness, whenever a lost candle saw their light, it no longer was lost.

Easy Object Lesson

Let an unopened folding chair crash to a carpeted floor. Say, "This Christian tried to stand on her own two legs without the support of other Christians." Pick the chair up and open it. Say, "Other Christians (represented by the spread legs) could have held her up." If you wish, add to the front of the chair's back rest (the side toward the audience when the chair falls) giant wiggle eyes, a pompon nose, a frowning paper mouth, and fake fur eyebrows. Decorate the other side with smiling features. You may want to put fake fur hair on the top of the back rest (seen from either side).

Puppet Talk

Show a glove puppet (see pp. 94-5) as a candle with a cardboard flame and use a cardboard candleholder (figure 1A, audience's view; figure 1B, side view). After first showing the puppet, remove the flame from its mouth so it can speak.

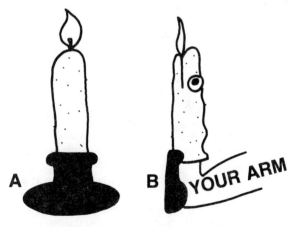

Figure 1   **Puppet Talk**

Chalk Talk

See figure 2.

Figure 2 **Chalk Talk**

3

You Are Special

Even the very hairs of your head are all numbered. (Matt.
10:30)

Freddie Frog was just an ugly little lump; he wasn't hand-some, he wasn't a football star, and he wasn't smart. But he needed to feel special. So he drew a picture of a handsome frog with huge muscles on top of muscles. On it he wrote,

FREDDIE THE SUPERFROG

"Whatcha drawin?" asked Billy Bull.

Then he snatched the picture away from Freddie.

"Look kids!" he screamed. "Freddie thinks he's a super-frog." And they all laughed so hard they rolled on the floor.

That really made Freddie feel like a worm, a nothing. He cried so many tears on the school bus on the way home that the driver had to stop and open the door four times to let the water out.

At home he read in the paper about a home for crippled children who didn't feel special either.

"Those poor kids feel like worms, too," said Freddie. "I'm going to make them feel special."

So in his spare time, he went to the home and taught the children games. With hugs and love he would say, "My, you run fast!" "What pretty brown eyes you have!" "You did great!" "You're a very special person."

One day there was a knock at his door. He opened it to see a group of the crippled children. Giving him a huge bouquet of roses, which cost them all the money they had, they said, "God bless you, Freddie! You made us feel special. So we love you very, very much."

After they left, Freddie cried for joy. He knew that being a football star or being handsome meant nothing in God's eyes. Over and over he shouted, "I'm special because I can show love!"

Easy Object Lesson

Make imaginary measurements with a ruler, yardstick, tape, etc. Then say, "People are always measuring and comparing each other." Hold up a paper heart and say, "But each person is special because he is special to God and because he can show love."

Puppet Talk

Stick brown paper legs and a large wiggle eye on your fist (figure 1). Measure the frog and use the heart as in the easy object lesson.

← **YOUR SLEEVE**

Figure 1 **Puppet Talk**

Figure 2   **Chalk Talk**

Chalk Talk

See figure 2. The tag can be a predrawn cutout and stuck on. Use a measuring device and a heart as in the easy object lesson.

4
Do-What-I-Want Day*

*Look out for one another's interests, not just for your own.
(Phil. 2:4 TEV)*

Dickie Duck lived with his family in a box. It was a box of quackers. One day he said, "Aw, Mom, I don't wanna do the dishes. Tomorrow let's have a Do-What-I-Want Day."

"Okay," she said.

That night he dreamed it was a national Do-What-I-Want Day. When he asked his mom to get his breakfast, she said, "I don't wanna!"

Then he saw his little sister Maggie hogging his favorite cereal.

"Hey, Shovel Mouth," he said, "save some for me."

"I don't wanna," said Maggie.

So Dickie pulled her feathers and made her bawl. Then he ate some candy until it came out of his ears, giving him a tummy ache and sticky ears.

Nothing worked that day—Dickie didn't have a phone, newspaper, or TV because nobody wanted to work. People couldn't even drive anywhere because of the all-day traffic jams at stop lights: nobody wanted to obey the signals.

With his tummy ache, Dickie had to walk four miles and two inches to the doctor's office. But there a sign said,

SORRY SICKIES, THE DOCTOR DIDN'T WANT TO WORK.

Then Dickie woke up. He ran into his parent's bedroom crying, "Please don't have a Do-What-I-Want Day tomorrow.

*This idea is from a story by Margaret Tappan in *Presbyterian Life*, June 22, 1957.

Figure 1 **Puppet Talk**

Figure 2 **Chalk Talk**

Doing what I want all the time is selfish, and that's no fun at all."

Easy Object Lesson

Stagger under the load of a paper crown, labeled "KING ME," on your head.

Puppet Talk

Form a Z with your arm (figure 1) and put a 1″ wiggle eye on the side of your index finger at the knuckle so that your hand looks like a duck.

Chalk Talk

See figure 2.

5
Holding Back Part of Your Heart

Love the Lord your God with all your heart. (Matt. 22:37)

Tommy's friend Chris had something wonderful—faith in Jesus. Tommy wanted this too, so he prayed, "Dear Lord, I give You my heart—well most of it." He wanted to hang on to a few bad thoughts in a tiny bit of his heart. *Surely this wouldn't make any difference*, he thought. But deep down inside he knew he had to be honest with Jesus.

Later he was teaching his little brother Tad to swim. Tad splashed with one hand and kicked so hard his bow legs looked like an eggbeater. But his other hand clung to the pool's edge.

Tommy said, "Tad, if you don't trust yourself completely to the water, you'll never swim."

Then a thought struck Tommy, "I lack trust, too. I must trust Jesus completely as a wonderful Friend whose way is best." Then he found the joy and peace of having Jesus live in his heart by praying, "Dear Lord, I give You all of my heart."

Easy Object Lesson

Tear a piece off of a white paper heart before giving it to God (putting it on the altar). Later, restore with tape the piece to the heart to show complete commitment. One side of the heart is dirty, while the other side contains a picture of Jesus, or a cross (to show that now Jesus lives there).

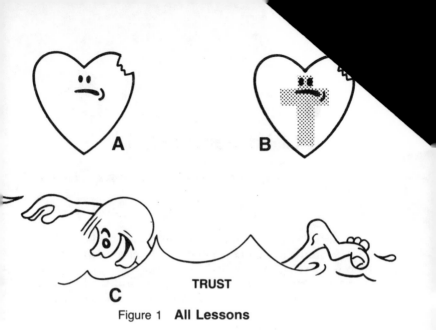

Figure 1 **All Lessons**

Fun Object Lesson

Follow the instructions for the easy object lesson, but put the heart on some bathroom scales ("which evaluate hearts") placed on the altar. From under the scales, remove a card saying "0" ("before total commitment") and a card saying "100%" ("after total commitment"). Or use "talking scales" (a tape recorder lying on its back) to give a cheer and fanfare.

Puppet Talk

Follow the instructions for the easy object lesson, but remove the heart from under the puppet's skirt.

Chalk Talk

See figure 1. Draw the sad heart (A), then the swimmer (C), then draw in the missing piece and cover up the sad expression with a cross (B).

21

hild Serves God

Here is a boy with five small barley loaves and two small fish. (John 6:9)

(Ask the children what they can do for God.)

The animals decided to make a flower garden for God. The enormous elephant pulled up trees; the mighty ox plowed; but Molly Mouse sobbed, "I'm only six and too little to help."

One day she saw a sign on the garden land saying,

FUTURE HOME OF THE BRISTLELESS BRUSH COMPANY.
WE MAKE BARE BRUSHES FOR BALDIES.

The animals must have given up the garden!

Molly ran to the elephant and demanded, "Why did you give up God's garden?"

"We're too big and clumsy to plant itty bitty seeds," he said.

"Well," said Molly, "I'll plant some seeds around my home in the field."

The other little animals also planted seeds around their homes in the field. Soon a lovely garden grew, and the animals had a party to thank the workers. Molly went to watch the elephant and the other important adults be honored for big jobs. But, to her surprise, when she entered the room everyone cheered. "Hurray for Molly! Hurray! Hurray! There would be no garden if you hadn't planted your small corner."

You see, everyone's work is equally important to God, even the work done by a small child.

Easy Object Lesson

A seed packet or fake (paper wad) seeds.

Figure 1 **Fun Object Lesson**

Fun Object Lesson

Look like a mouse by sticking a black paper nose on your nose and paper ears, cut from a grocery bag, on your ears. At first, bow your head, suck in your cheeks, hold your hands as

Figure 2 **Puppet Talk**

23

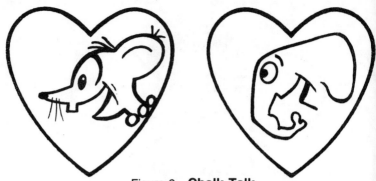

Figure 3 **Chalk Talk**

shown (figure 1A) and dart your eyes about like a timid mouse. Turn the mouse into an elephant by holding a big work sock (elephant's trunk) up to your nose, keeping the mouse ears in place.

Puppet Talk

Put your left thumb, which is inside a dark sock, against the crotch of your right thumb and forefinger (figure 2). Stick paper ears and eyes on the mouse and wiggle it.

Chalk Talk

See figure 3. Hold paper hearts to your eyes and say, "In God's loving eyes, the service of the mouse and elephant were of equal value."

7
Discouraged Cloud

Give thanks whatever happens. (1 Thess. 5:18 NEB)

Discouraged Christians are poor Christians because they don't feel like doing much for God. And Discouraged Cloud did nothing but cry a lot of rain. Clouds lose weight when they cry; and he was almost down to thin air.

Then a bird, singing at the top of his lungs, flew into Discouraged Cloud for a bath.

"Quiet, Squeaky Beak!" roared Discouraged Cloud. "You give me a headache."

"I can't help singing, you misty mess," said the bird. "Thanking God for anything and everything makes me feel good all over. That's what's wrong with you—no thanksgiving."

So Discouraged Cloud feebly prayed, "God, thanks for this pesky ol' bird."

Discouraged Cloud praised God until his discouragement vanished. And soon he was a gorgeous pink, smiling in the setting sun.

Easy Object Lesson

At the proper times in the story, show the black and pink sides of a paper cloud.

Fun Object Lesson

Add wiggle eyes and a frowning mouth to the paper cloud's dark side (see easy object lesson), and wiggle eyes, a smile, and the word "PRAISE" to its pink side. As one hand removes the

Figure 1 **Chalk Talk**

cloud from a bucket on a chair, your other hand removes a wet sponge hidden behind the cloud. Squeeze the sponge to make the cloud cry into the bucket. To secretly get rid of the sponge, hold the cloud close to the bucket and drop the sponge into it. Turn the cloud from the dark side to the light side at the proper time.

Puppet Talk

Show an envelope puppet bird (see page 95). Combine the fun object lesson with the puppet talk.

Chalk Talk

Draw the cloud, then the bird. Invert the cloud to make it smile (figure 1).

8
Links

Preserve the unity which the Spirit gives. (Eph. 4:3 TEV)

Once Charlie Chain said, "I hate being in a water well chain. I quit."

So he left the chain, leaving it missing a link. Then he did nothing but hang around with a bad chain gang. He refused to be linked to anything, not even the church. But if he really loved the Lord he would want to worship with the Lord's friends.

Chain links have no muscles when they aren't connected, so Charlie was too weak to lift anything. He was so weak and worthless that he visited his old chain to keep from being bored. There he saw a thirsty little girl crying beside the useless broken chain that couldn't pull the water bucket up from the well. Quickly Charlie took his place in the chain so the girl could get a drink.

Then he realized that if Christians aren't linked into a church, the world would be a mess. They must work together as God's chain to draw people to Himself. He told the rest of the chain, "Hey, I'm part of a chain in God's hands. And that's exciting!"

Easy Object Lesson

Show two paper chains and a detached link, Charlie Chain, who later links the two chains together. *Options:* Draw or glue a face on Charlie and use masking tape to close him. At one end of the chain is Christ's picture. At the other end is a magazine or catalog picture of several people. Say, "We must link people to Christ."

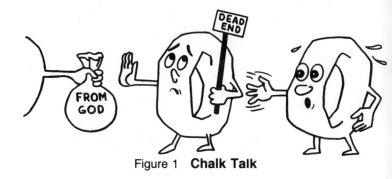

Figure 1 **Chalk Talk**

Chalk Talk

See figure 1. Save time by predrawing the figures on the left and right.

9

The Wonderful Friend

In Christ ... you have been brought to completion. (Col. 2:9-10 *NEB*)

A half pair of scissors, named Half-There, felt like a sheep without a shepherd. Knowing something was missing in his life, he tried everything to find it.

He tried wealth, making zillions of dollars selling shoes to centipedes. Still something was missing.

He tried fame, jumping off a roof of a skyscraper to set a world's record for breaking the most bones. A bunch of cheering idiots put him on TV. Still something was missing.

He tried popularity, going to a dog show wearing a huge badge saying "CONTEST JUDGE." The dogs fell all over him and made him more popular than a fried fish at a cat convention. Still something was missing.

Finally, he felt so badly that he read his Maker's instruction book, the Bible, where Jesus said, "I am the good shepherd. The good shepherd lays down his life for the sheep" (John 10:11).

"Hooray!" shouted Half-There. "Nobody else loves me like that. Jesus is my wonderful Friend who's missing from my life." So he gave his heart to Jesus and knew that at last he was complete.

Easy Object Lesson

Grip a scissors handle in one hand and its blade in the other so only the other half of the scissors shows. Reveal the full scissors at the right time.

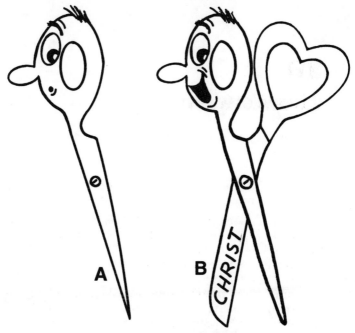

Figure 1　**Chalk Talk**

Fun Object Lesson

To illustrate Half-There, hide one side of your face and upper body by draping a dark coat over one side of your face and body and briefly standing on one leg.

Puppet Talk

From under the puppet's skirt, remove a heart folded down the middle to look like half a heart. Later, open it up.

Chalk Talk

See figure 1. Draw A, then complete the scissors (B), covering the wistful mouth with a smile.

10
Givers Receive

Give, and it will be given to you. (Luke 6:38)

Polly the pansy snarled, "Nobody but nobody's gonna pick my flower. It's all mine." She hid her face under the grass among the creepy crawlers. Soon her flower shriveled and fell off. Selfish people always shrivel up inside.

But another flower, Joy, waved her head up high saying, "Look! Pick me!"

And a wee girl laughed and said, "See the pretty flower!" She picked it and gave it to her mommy. How happy Mommy looked.

A few days later something wonderful happened: Joy grew a new flower, like some flowers do.

Next a worried old man picked Joy's flower, put it in his lapel, and looked happy. The more Joy's flowers were picked, the more they grew back, spreading joy everywhere. And Joy was the happiest flower you can imagine. When you give joy, you have it yourself.

Easy Object Lesson

Throw quarter-moon shaped red cardboard "smiles" around the room, saying, "Joy scattered happiness."

Fun Object Lesson

Fold a big blue paper square as shown (figure 1A-D), cutting off the shaded area in D. Tape this flower to the back of your fist, adding wiggle eyes and a paper mouth to the bare center of your fist (E). Hold this flower low and wiggle your other

31

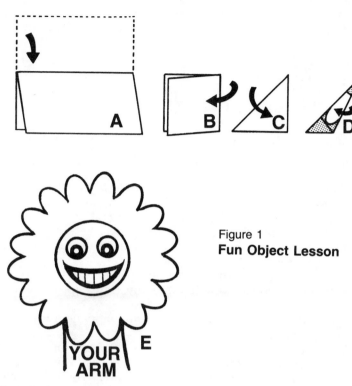

Figure 1
Fun Object Lesson

hand's fingers over it ("Creepy crawlers ran over Polly."). Then wave the flower up high and blow on it ("Joy waved in the breeze.").

Puppet Talk

Frame a puppet's head with a circle of paper petals (see above) and pin several paper leaves to the puppet's body.

Chalk Talk

Change the story to say, "The old man put Joy in a vase on a round table" (see figure 2A). Complete the drawing (figure 2B) and say, "See how happy Joy made the old man."

A

Figure 2 **Chalk Talk**

B

11
Be Yourself

There are different ways of serving ... the same LORD.
(1 Cor. 12:5 TEV)

"I'm a dinky little nothing," moaned Perry Parrot in the pet shop. "If only I were a scary lion, people would buy me to guard their homes." And he wrapped a green dust mop around his neck like a lion's mane.

He tried to roar to impress a lady customer; but all he did was cough his head off. And the lady said, "What's that horrid green seaweed doing in the parrot cage?"

Next Perry tried to be an elephant by sticking an old sock on his nose like an elephant's trunk. But a customer said, "What's that? It looks like a worm and smells like athlete's foot."

Then the shop owner scolded Perry, "You can't improve on being yourself. God loves you just the way you are."

So, in his best parrot voice, Perry said, "Polly wants a cracker." And a dozen customers ran to his cage yelling, "That's just what I want, a parrot."

Easy Object Lesson

At the proper times in the story wrap fuzzy material (mop head, throw rug, sweater, towel) around your neck, and put a sock on your nose.

Puppet Talk

Put the green material and sock on a bird puppet (see pages 94-5).

34

Figure 1 **Chalk Talk**

Chalk Talk

See figure 1. Draw the parrot and hold up green material and a sock to it. At the end, use red chalk to cross out "NOT" and make an exclamation mark after "OK."

12

How to See God

Blessed are the pure in heart, for they will see God.
(Matt. 5:8)

"Pussycat, Pussycat, where have you been?"

"I've been to London to see the queen."

"Pussycat, Pussycat, what did you there?"

"I frightened a little mouse under her chair."

When Pussy got home—she lives next to me—her mother excitedly asked, "So what was the queen like?"

"Dunno," said Pussycat. "But I scared the daylights out of an ol' mouse."

"Phooey!" snorted her mother. "One sees only what is important to her. A bird would see a worm; a donkey, hay; a politician, voters. You didn't even notice the queen; all you saw was a mouse!"

Pussycat started to cry.

"Don't feel badly, dear," said her mother. "You can see something better than the queen. If God is the most important thing in your life, you can see Him in the sky and the flowers, in people's faces, and in everything good and beautiful."

That night I heard a horrible yowling outside my window and yelled, "Quiiii-yut!"

"Sorry," said Pussycat, "I was only saying my prayers."

"Praying for a mouse, I suppose," I said.

"No, asking God to be the most important thing in my life," she replied.

Easy Object Lesson

Hold small paper hearts over your eyes and say, "Our hearts control what we see."

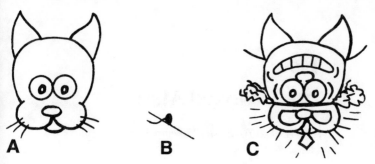

Figure 1   **Chalk Talk**

Fun Object Lesson

Show the queen by sticking a two-dimensional yellow paper crown on your forehead and say, "But all Pussycat saw was a mouse." (Make yourself into a mouse. See p. 23–4).

Puppet Talk

Put the paper hearts (see the easy object lesson) over a cat puppet's eyes (see p. 91).

Chalk Talk

See figure 1. Draw a cat (A) ("which saw a mouse"). Draw a mouse tail going into a hole (B). Add lines to the cat (C), and invert it to show the queen.

13

The Crooked Man

The crooked roads shall become straight. *(Luke 3:5)*

There was a crooked man, and he went a crooked mile.
He found a crooked sixpence against a crooked stile;
He bought a crooked cat, which caught a crooked mouse.
And they all lived together in a little crooked house.

Actually things only looked crooked to the man because he had a crooked heart. The attitude of the heart controls how one sees things. People look like lemons to sour people, like mud to dirty people, like mules to stubborn people.

Mr. Crooked tried to be a sign painter, but he made his letters crooked. His *I*s looked like *Z*s. And he drove his car crookedly down straight roads, crashing into trees.

He cheated everyone. Once he even cheated himself, got mad and beat himself up. Pow! Pow! Whang! Bang! "Ouchity, ouch!" And an ambulance, siren screaming and lights flashing, rushed him to the hospital. There he turned cross-eyed, and his eyes as well as the rest of his body ached like a saw with a toothache in every tooth. So he screamed so loud he blew his bed sheets into the hall.

Two doctors ran to Mr. Crooked, examined him, and said, "Your eyes hurt from seeing evil in people because your heart is crooked. Only Jesus can straighten crooked things."

So Mr. Crooked gave his heart to Jesus. Then people called him Mr. Straight, and he saw good in everyone.

All Lessons

Hold a mirror to your face (or to a puppet or drawing). Say, "The crooked man saw his own faults in others."

Figure 1 **Fun Object Lesson**

Fun Object Lesson

Make a man from a grocery bag. Cut and assemble four 3" x 17" pieces (limbs) and one 7" x 17" piece (head and body) folded at odd angles (see figure 1). Add feet and slits for fingers. Add a 2" pink pompon nose, 1-1/2" wiggle eyes, fake fur hair, and a red mouth. Shake hands with this man and act like he is real.

Puppet Talk

Pin a crooked paper body (see fun object lesson) to a puppet, so the puppet head serves as the body's head.

Figure 2 **Chalk Talk**

Chalk Talk

Draw the crooked man (figure 2), adding his worn-out hat last. Invert the picture and say, "When he was stubborn, he looked like a mule."

14

The Lady
with the Beautiful Face

Men judge by appearances but the LORD judges by the heart. (1 Sam. 16:7 NEB)

You never heard such a racket in all your life. Fighting, kicking, scratching, biting, hair pulling! It was a beauty contest. In last place came Ruthie, so ugly she curdled milk.

In tears she ran to the drug store yelling, "Gimme all the thick face paint, eye gook, beauty cream, and mud packs you got. I want my hair curled and my teeth polished. I wanna be gorgeous."

"Sorry," said the clerk. "For you, that would be a miracle. That stuff only hides your outsides; true beauty is in the heart."

"Okay, give me a miracle," said Ruthie.

The clerk sold her a huge box labeled "SUPER MIRACLE FOR UGLIES." Inside the box a tiny slip of paper said, "Smile. Be kind and loving."

So Ruthie smiled to cheer up sad people. And she became everyone's friend, helping everyone who had a problem.

Did this work? Well, twenty years later everyone in town called Ruthie "the lady with the beautiful face."

All Lessons

Show some beauty aids and tell what they do. Then show a paper heart and say, "True beauty comes from within."

Object Lesson

Present a plastic milk jug with 1-1/2" wiggle eyes and a paper mouth and tongue stuck on it (figure 1). Sniff the bottle and make a sick face (grabbing your throat and sticking out your tongue) or pretend to almost faint. Say, "Ruthie was so ugly she curdled milk."

Puppet Talk

Remove a paper heart from under the puppet's skirt and say, "Beauty comes from within." Pretend to put beauty aids on the puppet's face.

Chalk Talk

See figure 2. Draw the dog (A), changing the story to say, "Ugly Ruthie looked like a dog." Add lines (B) and invert— "Ruthie became gorgeous."

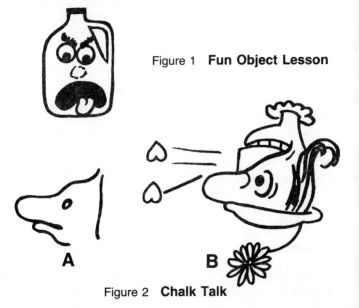

Figure 1 **Fun Object Lesson**

Figure 2 **Chalk Talk**

15

The Inside Out Porcupine

If you do not forgive men their sins, your Father will not forgive your sins. (Matt. 6:15)

One morning Willie Worm phoned Perry Porcupine and said, "Sorry, but I broke your pen that I borrowed."

"What! You busted my birthday present!" Perry yelled so loudly that the phone wires outside heated up, giving the birds on them the hotfoot.

Perry Porcupine was so angry that he put on his porcupine skin inside out. Oooh! That must have hurt. He couldn't eat because chewing made the needles stick to his face. He couldn't sit down because it hurt to sit on the needles. He couldn't lie down because that hurt worse. He couldn't scratch his back because that made the needles hurt his back. He couldn't do his homework because all he could think about was his pain. Even when he put his porcupine suit on right side out he still hurt. He had to stand up to ride the school bus.

On the school bus, Perry grabbed Willie Worm's lunch money and threw it out of the bus window. Willie cried because he hadn't had any breakfast as his family was terribly poor.

When Perry saw Willie crying he felt ashamed of himself. And he realized that what people did to him couldn't hurt him at all. It was his own mean feelings that were hurting him.

He put his arm around Willie and said, "I forgive you for breaking my pen. And, at the school cafeteria, I'm going to buy you the best lunch you ever had."

Willie smiled from ear to ear. And then and there Perry's mean feelings went away.

Easy Object Lesson

Stick an eye on a hairbrush and call it a porcupine (figure 1).

Figure 1 **Easy Object Lesson**

Fun Object Lesson

Use a shag throw rug, fur coat, or bath towel as the porcupine skin. Say, "Perry kept his quills sharp" and pretend to sharpen a "quill" with a file. Test that quill with your finger, say "Ouch!" and put a Band-Aid or bandage on your finger. Wrap the "porcupine skin" inside out around you and squirm saying, "Ouch! Ouch! Ouch! That hurts!"

Figure 2 **Chalk Talk**

Puppet Talk

Follow the instructions for the fun object lesson, but wrap fake fur or fuzzy material around a puppet.

Chalk Talk

See figure 2.

16
On the Enemy Team

He who is not with me is against me, and he who does not gather with me scatters.   (Matt. 12:30)

When Felix Fish read about Jesus he said, "He's my hero. Someday I'll be a missionary and help Him."

And Felix was Gus Guppy's hero. He and his friends followed Felix one Sunday when Felix was a man-er-fish. It's the opposite of a fisherman. You bait a fishing line with five-dollar bills and try to catch a man.

The instant Felix got home that Sunday, his phone rang like crazy. When Felix answered it, he heard Gus Guppy's mom sob and plead, "Please, please go to church; my boy copies you."

"Aw, I'm a good guy without going to church all the time," said Felix.

Gus's mom replied, "But if you loved the Lord, you would want to be in His house. Jesus said, 'He who isn't for me is against me.' If your example doesn't lead others to Him, it leads them away."

"Phooey," said Felix. "It's my own business."

The next day a package came to Felix in the mail, a cloth letter D, like school athletes wear.

"Yippee!" yelled Felix. "I'll stick it on my back for all the girls to admire."

Then he read the letter that came with it:

Dear Felix,
    Congrats! You made my first team. Your example sure helps me. Every time you miss church you encourage others to do it.
                       The Devil.

Easy Object Lesson

Remove a paper letter D from an envelope.

Puppet Talk

Use a novelty quickie fish puppet (See p. 93).

Chalk Talk

See figure 1.

Figure 1 **Chalk Talk**

17

Less Is More

He trims any branch that bears fruit to make it bear more fruit.   (John 15:2 Beck)

Holly Garden Hose sprang a leak here and a leak there to water dandelions, thinking it was fun. Water spilled out all over the place. Finally the water at Holly's nozzle trickled so weakly it would take a mosquito a month to get enough to brush its teeth. And the flowers in God's garden that Holly should have watered turned a sick, shriveled brown.

One day, Holly heard a horrible rumble: growl, growl, growl! [Make a noise like a truck motor.] It came from the garbage truck, which roared, "I'm gonna get you. I'm gonna get you." [Laugh like a fiend.] "I saw the Master Gardener looking in a catalog for a new hose. He's gonna give you the old heave ho. Ya better straighten up, kid."

Holly was so scared that she tied herself into knots. "Oh, dear, what can I do?" she cried.

The truck replied, "Get ridda your leaks. You gotta give up extra things to have power for the Lord. Some people give up extra meetings or too much TV."

So Holly patched her leaks. And a mighty stream of water shot out her nozzle. Whoosh! Soon God's garden bloomed, a riot of red, yellow, blue, and purple. Holly was happier than she had ever been before, and she didn't even miss watering dandelions.

Easy Object Lesson

Crumple some papers (labeled or pictured with distractions, such as "TOO MUCH TV") and throw them into a wastebasket. Say, "A Christian must get rid of everything standing between him and Jesus."

Fun Object Lesson

With hedge trimmers or scissors, trim and throw into a wastebasket branches sticking out of many pockets in your clothes. Or do the above with paper branches or with pictures and labels of distractions pinned to your clothes.

Puppet Talk

Follow the instructions for the fun object lesson, pinning the above cited items to a puppet.

Chalk Talk

See figure 1. Draw the faded grass and a bee (A) and say, "The garden looked sad; and even the bees looked sad because there were no flowers." Add the lines in B and say, "Now everyone was happy. The flowers looked happy. The bees looked happy. And even the garbage truck driver looked like this."

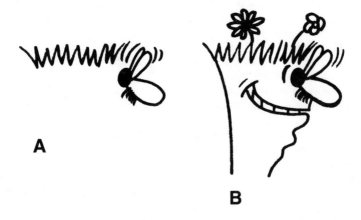

Figure 1   **Chalk Talk**

18
Finger Sandwich

We are members one of another.   *(Eph. 4:25 RSV)*

Daphne Dachshund was a mean dog. Her body was so long that when she walked around a tree she would see her tail in front of her and think it was another dog.

Who's that slowpoke dog in front of me? she would think. And she would get mad and put salt and paper on the tail in front of her, bite down hard on it, and yell, "Ouch!" She never could figure out why her own tail hurt when she did the biting. It was like eating a finger sandwich [see the easy object lesson]. Then she got so boiling mad that when she drank water it blew out of her ears as steam. What a hot dog she was! Her body got so hot it cooked her leather collar tender enough to eat. And her hair got frizzy and started to burn and smell awful.

The smell made her neighbor, Polly Poodle, as sick as a dog. Finally when Daphne was asleep, Polly tied a sign on her tail that said, "I LOVE YOU."

The next time Daphne walked around a tree, she thought she saw another dog's tail in front of her with a sign saying, "I LOVE YOU."

What a nice dog that is in front of me! she thought. The tail looked sore from being bitten, so Daphne put some soothing medicine on it instead of biting it. Then she felt good instead of hurting. Suddenly she realized that God made us to be a part of each other. We feel bad when we think mean thoughts about others and good when we think good thoughts about them. So Daphne decided never ever to think mean thoughts again.

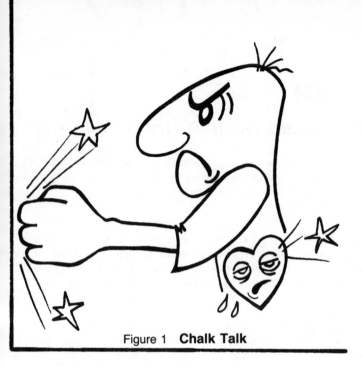

Figure 1 **Chalk Talk**

Easy Object Lesson

When the story mentions a finger sandwich, make one: stick the fingers of one hand between two pieces of bread, bite down, and yell, "Ouch!" *Options:* Pretend to spread the bread with ketchup, mustard, peanut butter, anything else you can think of. Use the real products or fake it, using empty containers.

Puppet Talk

Follow the instructions for the easy object lesson, using a puppet.

Chalk Talk

"When we hit someone else we make our own hearts sad." (See figure 1.)

19
Love Power *(Christmas Story)*

For God so loved the world that he gave his one and only Son, that whoever believes in him shall not perish but have eternal life. *(John 3:16)*

Toby was born with a huge ugly birthmark on his face. All the kids made fun of him and he acted mean in return. At his high school graduation party, the class president, Wilfred Q. Smathers, said, "I nominate Toby as the one of us most likely to be ugly." Everyone laughed. But Toby ran home, red faced and terribly hurt.

That night he heard a knock at his door. But no one was there, only a basket holding a crying baby with an ugly purple mark on its face, just like Toby's. He looked at the tiny hands and face and thought, *He's so helpless, I just have to take care of him and teach him not to be ashamed of his face.*

For the first time in his life, Toby felt needed. His whole life changed and he got even with his classmates by doing good things for them. Eventually his face glowed with such kindness and love that he looked beautiful. And all because a helpless baby led him to Jesus. Babies teach us to love. That's why Jesus came to earth as a helpless baby.

Years later, Toby attended his class's thirtieth anniversary dinner. Wilfred Q. Smathers stood up and said, "I nominate Toby as the one of us who's the most like Jesus." And do you know what? Everyone stood up and cheered!

Easy Object Lesson

Roll up a towel or baby blanket to look like it holds a baby (whose face isn't shown to the audience). Or show a doll wrapped up in the blanket, or show a picture of a baby.

Puppet Talk

See figure 1. In front of the audience, use markers to draw blue eyes, a faint red nose, and a red mouth on the back of one of your hands. Put your hand on a towel (B; one side of the towel is shaded only to help you keep track of the sides). Wrap your knuckles in the blanket (C) and throw it over your arm (D). E shows how the baby will look. It can wiggle, turn its head, or bounce when you tickle its tummy. (Illustrations A and E are the audience's view while B-D are your view of the hand in front of you. X-X indicates the segment of cloth that crosses over your knuckles.

Chalk Talk

See figure 2. Comment on how the baby Jesus is an expression of God's love.

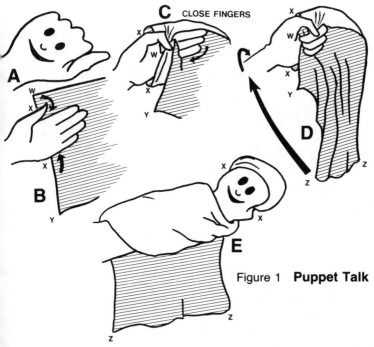

Figure 1 **Puppet Talk**

53

Figure 2 **Chalk Talk**

20

Prune or Hero?

Store up for yourselves treasures in heaven. (Matt. 6:20)

One night in bed, Tracy heard a little voice crying, "Help! Help! Helpity, help!"

He looked all around the room but saw nothing. "Who are you?" he asked.

"Your soul," said the voice, "and I'm starving to death."

"Impossible!" said Tracy. "I eat like a horse."

"Don't tell me you eat hay," said his soul. "You feed your body, but I'm starving. When your life is over and you meet God, do you want a shriveled prune soul?"

"Certainly not," said Tracy. "Souls are terribly important. What kind of food do you need?"

"Prayer, praise, Bible reading, church attendance, and good deeds are my food," said his soul.

At this Tracy was so bothered that he got up in the middle of the night to pray. His wife had never seen him pray, so she thought he must be dying.

"Yikes!" she screamed. "Don't you dare die! It might be bad for your health!"

"Don't worry," said Tracy, "I'm in good health and my soul is going to be healthy, too."

He began feeding his soul regularly and the next time it spoke to him it was a big, strong, beautiful hero soul.

Easy Object Lesson

From under your coat, remove a tiny crumpled heart ("Tracy's shriveled soul") cut from a grocery bag. Hold this heart between your thumb and index finger tips and make a face. Then remove from your coat a giant white paper heart (made

from six pieces of typing paper glued together) with a red mouth and the word "HERO" in red (Tracy's hero soul, figure 1). An alternative idea is to show how Tracy fed his body by tilting back your head, sticking a funnel in your mouth, and pretending (keep the lids on the bottles) to pour milk and pop into the funnel at once. Then with a fork or spoon in each hand, shovel imaginary food into the funnel as fast as you can.

Puppet Talk

Follow the instructions for the easy object lesson, but remove the hearts from the puppet's skirt.

Chalk Talk

Say that Tracy had a shriveled tramp soul and draw the tramp. Then draw the crown to show that Tracy had gained a hero soul.

Figure 1 **Easy Object Lesson**

Interior lines indicate arrangement of six pieces of typing paper glued together.

Figure 2 **Chalk Talk**

21

You Harvest What You Plant

Whatever you sow you'll reap. (Gal. 6:7 Beck)

When mean Gomer Goat saw his reflection in a store mirror, he thought it was another goat and made a face at it. [Make a funny face.] The mirror made the same face back, so he made another face. [Make another one.] The mirror did the same. He shook his fist. So did the mirror. Then he butted the mirror so hard that his head went right through the wall out into the street and got stuck there. Thinking his head in the wall was a pay phone, people began stuffing quarters down his throat. It was awful: he weighed a ton before he finally jerked his head loose.

By then Gomer had figured out that when he was mean all his meanness came back to him. So he decided to try being nice.

Just then a little girl skipped by with an ice-cream cone. She tripped and spilled her ice cream on the sidewalk. Then she cried like her heart would break. So Gomer bought her another ice-cream cone.

Later he ran home in joy. "Mom," he yelled, "the nicest thing happened to me. A little girl gave me a great big hug and kiss."

Easy Object Lesson

Show a mirror. Stick a wiggle eye and a cotton beard (or any kind of fuzz) on a hammer to make a goat (see figure 1). Make butting motions with it to show it knocking people.

Puppet Talk

Use a novelty quickie goat puppet (see p. 93).

Chalk Talk

See figure 2.

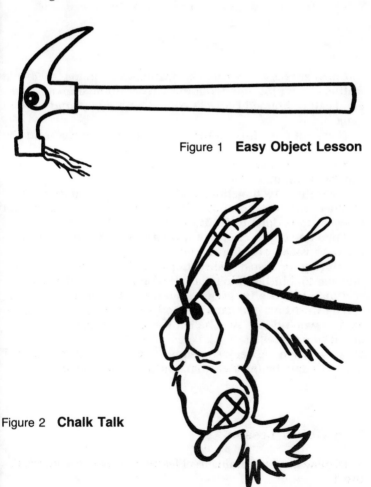

Figure 1 **Easy Object Lesson**

Figure 2 **Chalk Talk**

22

Tough Guys Aren't Copycats

Be brave, be strong.   (1 Cor. 16:13 TEV)

Copycat was a toy cat with feathers for brains. As a rule feathers aren't too smart, but these were dumb even for feathers. Feather brained Copycat copied anything stupid his bad gang did.

"Let's hit ourselves on the head with a hammer," said the gang. "Come on, Copycat, be like us tough guys."

So Copycat hit himself on the head. But he didn't like himself for doing it.

Then the gang took dope and one of them died from it and another one lost his mind. How stupid can you get? And Copycat took dope too. But he didn't like himself.

Then one day in church, Copycat heard how Jesus died on a cross instead of being scared by a tough gang.

"Hurray for Jesus!" yelled Copycat right in church. Everyone stared, but he didn't care. He'd learned that Jesus was a real man because He wasn't scared of what people thought.

The next time the gang wanted Copycat to do wrong, he said, "I won't do it!" And he left the gang. At last he felt good about himself.

Now, when he sees someone copy a bad gang, Copycat says, "I know better than that, and I'm only a feather brain."

Easy Object Lesson

Display the cat's brains (real feathers or paper features, figure 1).

Figure 1   **Easy Object Lesson**

Fun Object Lesson

Tape a cat nose and jaw (cut from a bag and outlined in black, figure 2) onto your face. With your fingers, pull your eyes into slats when you first show the cat. *Optional:* Tape an envelope labeled "CAT BRAINS," to your forehead and remove feathers from it.

Figure 2   **Fun Object Lesson**

Puppet Talk

See cat puppet on page 91.

Chalk Talk

See figure 3. Instead of a cat, make the story hero a feather-brained boy who acted like a chicken (A). At the story's end say, "He no longer acted like a chicken." Add the lines in B and invert to show a brave boy.

Figure 3 **Chalk Talk**

23

Near to God

The LORD is near to all who call on him. (Ps. 145:18)

Sam, the ham radio, had a terribly sick plastic leg. Ant-sized termites with elephant-sized appetites were eating it up. (The termites thought his leg was wooden. Dumb termites!) When Sam tuned in to God to pray for help, He seemed millions of miles away.

Sam went to the hospital about his leg; and the doctors said, "Hmm. Hmm. Looks bad. Hurry into the operating room. We'll try to save it."

Sam prayed more than ever on the way to the operating room. Now God only seemed thousands of miles away.

When Sam woke from the operation, the leg was gone. *Now what'll I do?* he thought. He prayed for help. The more he prayed the closer he felt to God. Finally he felt God's presence right inside his very heart. Sam was happier than he had ever been before.

When Sam's girl friend visited him in the hospital, she demanded, "So why didn't God answer your prayers?"

"Oh, but He did! He did!" said Sam. "He gave me the strength to get along without my leg. Sometimes true prayer brings what we seek, sometimes something better, but always it brings us closer to God. That's the real answer to prayer."

Easy Object Lesson

Show a radio.

Fun Object Lesson

Put a grocery bag (trimmed to reach from the top of your head to your shoulders) over your head. The bag should have

1-1/2" wiggle eyes, a white dial, a bright paper speaker, and an antenna made of a long narrow roll of paper (see figure 1). Hold a paper "radio wave" (see figure 2) in your extended hand and gradually move it closer until it's in Sam's heart (inside the bag) as he gets closer to God in prayer.

Puppet Talk

Instead of a radio, make the story hero a robot with an antenna (any puppet with a paper antenna pinned on it) that he uses to talk to God.

Chalk Talk

See figure 2. Draw the most distant radio wave and add them successively closer until you put one inside of Sam.

Figure 1 **Fun Object Lesson**

Figure 2 **Chalk Talk**

ur Mighty Mouth

Encourage . . . and build each other up. (1 Thess. 5:11)

With a tongue like a cactus, Cathy said such mean things that she made people feel bad about themselves.

Shy little Teri asked her, "How do you like my new red shoes, Cathy?" She was so proud of them.

"Red shoes look dumb," said Cathy.

Teri left in tears, feeling so small that she walked through the crack under the door.

"How'd she do that?" Cathy asked herself.

"That's how small you made her feel," said a mouse from a hole in the wall.

"Gracious!" said Cathy. "I never knew my tongue was so powerful."

From then on she said sweet things. She said things like, "That was a yummy breakfast, Mommy," and, "I wish I had a pretty smile like you, Teri."

Once, when Cathy was collecting lunch tickets at the school cafeteria, she said such nice things that all who went past her felt better about themselves. What a thrill it was for Cathy to see them all standing taller! She jumped up and turned three flips in midair, landing head first in a giant pot of mashed potatoes. But she didn't care, she was happy!

Easy Object Lesson

Tape a sign, saying "POWER" over your mouth. Remove the sign to talk. Say, "Our words have the power to make others feel good or bad."

Puppet Talk

Use a fist puppet (see p. 92) made by sticking your fist into a sock and putting wiggle eyes, a pompon nose, and a smiling paper mouth on the sock by your palm and frowning features at the back of your hand. By turning your wrist you can turn a mean, frowning Cathy into a kind, smiling Cathy.

Chalk Talk

See figure 1. Draw the cactus to illustrate Cathy's cactuslike tongue (A). Add the lines shown and invert (B). Say, "That looks like Cathy."

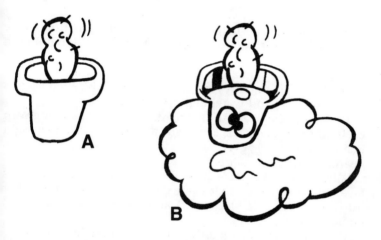

Figure 1   **Chalk Talk**

25

Vacuum Cleaner or Jewelry Box?

Fill your minds with those things that are good. (Phil. 4:8 TEV)

How many of you help your mothers vacuum? How many of you track in dirt for your mothers to vacuum? What does a vacuum cleaner eat? Dirt! It thinks dirt is yummy.

A girl named Velma had a vacuum-cleaner mind. She put rotten thoughts into it by hanging around with rotten friends and by reading and watching rotten things.

One night she heard the thoughts in her head arguing with each other. It made her sick; bad thoughts are enemies right inside your head. Everywhere she went this arguing was heard. How people stared!

After a while our faces look like our thoughts; and Velma's face looked so rotten that eight skinny vultures followed her into school, sat on a blackboard, and stared at her. Talk about embarrassing!

Velma was so ashamed that she started reading her Bible, praying, and thinking good things. Soon the vultures left, and her mind became a jewelry box full of beauty.

Easy Object Lesson

Show a vacuum cleaner, a vacuum bag, a dust ball or a jewelry box.

Figure 1 **Fun Object Lesson**

Fun Object Lesson

See figure 1. With an extension cord sticking from your pocket, a bright flattened paper cylinder in your mouth, and a grocery bag over your head (if necessary, tape the bag opening smaller to fit your head), make a gutteral hum like a vacuum cleaner. Remove the bag and pretend that it is full of dirt. Also show a jewelry box.

Puppet Talk

Follow the instructions for the easy object lesson, except make the puppet into a vacuum cleaner. Also show a jewelry box (see above).

Chalk Talk

See figure 2. Say, "Velma even began to look like a vacuum cleaner." (Draw her.) "Her mind became so rotten that flies and a vulture followed her into school." (Draw these things.) Show a jewelry box (see above) rather than drawing one.

Figure 2 **Chalk Talk**

26

Run from Temptation

Resist the devil, and he will flee from you. (James 4:7)

At the grocery store, Clean Clara met Dirty Dora, who said, "Let's steal some bananas. They have too many. They'll just rot anyway."

"Absotively, posilutely, no! Never!" said Clean Clara. "And what's more, I won't do it." Stealing looked wrong to her pure eyes.

But Dirty Dora kept begging and begging. And the more Clean Clara hung around her, the dirtier her eyes became. Finally it didn't seem wrong to take a couple of bananas. This they did, but the store owner saw them.

Dirty Dora stuck the bananas in her ears and said, "Moooo, mooooaw! I'm a cow with flabby yellow horns."

"Looks like bananas," said the store owner.

"So what?" said Dirty Dora. "I always wear bananas in my ears."

"I'm ashamed of you girls," said the owner.

Then Clara looked around. There stood her Sunday school class who had come to the store to buy her a birthday present. They had seen it all! Clara's face turned as red as a stop light.

Then Clara thought, *When I even listen to temptation, it dirties my eyes. The next time I see Dirty Dora, I'm going to run.*

All Lessons

Hold white and colored chalk together so the white chalk picks up some color. Say, "Contact with evil rubs off on us."

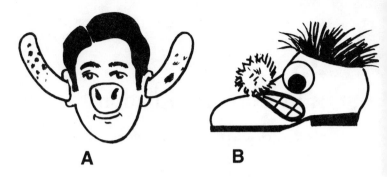

Figure 1 **Fun Object Lesson**

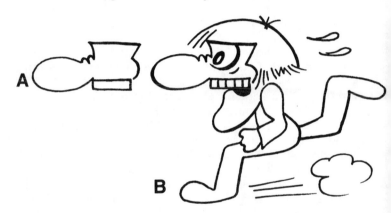

Figure 2 **Chalk Talk**

Easy Object Lesson

Display a bag and say, "In this bag is the way to face temptation." Then remove a shoe from the bag and say, "The way to handle temptation is to run from it."

Fun Object Lesson

See figure 1. Stick a paper cow's nose on your nose and hold yellow paper bananas to your ears ("Dora stuck the bananas in

her ears . . ." [A]). Show the shoe (as in the easy object lesson) with a 1-1/2″ wiggle eye stuck on it, a large pink pompon nose, a paper mouth, and fake fur hair (B).

Puppet Talk

Follow the instructions for the fun object lesson, sticking the cow's nose and bananas on a puppet instead of yourself.

Chalk Talk

See figure 2. Draw an old work shoe (A), then add the lines in B to show Clara running from temptation.

27

Starting Out
on the Wrong Foot

*On the Sabbath day [Jesus] went into the synagogue, as
was his custom.* (Luke 4:16)

After his parents left for church, Cedric Centipede thought,
*My bed feels so warm and comfy; it won't hurt if I miss church
just this once.*

But when he got up late, he no longer had his usual good
feeling of God's guiding presence. So he gave in to temptation
and looked in the cookie jar, even though his mother had told
him not to eat any cookies. He just smelled the cookies. Then
he ate just a crumb. Then he ate just one cookie. Then another
. . . and another . . . and another, until the jar was empty.

Cedric was afraid to face his parents, so he took a long walk
and just happened to run into a gang of bad boys. They
robbed a store, and he was only there watching, but the police
picked him up just the same.

When his parents came to get him out of jail, Cedric cried
and said, "I'm terribly sorry, Mom and Dad. But I only did one
thing wrong, and one thing kept leading to another. It's just
like my feet: if I start my front feet out right, the back ones will
follow."

From then on Cedric tried hard to start off the week right by
going to church.

Easy Object Lesson

Button a vest (or sweater) and end up wrong because you
started on the wrong button. *Optional:* Add 1-1/2" wiggle eyes, a
frowning paper mouth, and a pink pompon nose (prepared in
advance with tape loops) to the vest, to make a sad face.

Puppet Talk

Use an envelope centipede puppet (see pp. 94-5). Or make a centipede by sticking legs (bobby pins) through a puppet's sock body.

Chalk Talk

See figure 1.

Figure 1   **Chalk Talk**

28

Burden or Joy?

*Come to me, all you who are weary and burdened, and I
will give you rest.   (Matt. 11:28)*

Octavia Octopus's Bible said that Jesus is the Bread of Life.
So she wore zillions of bread wrappers on her eight arms and
carried around a huge hymn book. But the wrappers seemed
to weigh two tons. She didn't know that loving Jesus is a joy,
not a burden.

One day the wrappers got caught in some weeds and Octavia was stuck fast. "Help! Help! I'm gonna starve to death." She
screamed so loudly and made such giant waves that even the
whales got seasick.

Half a mile away, a fireman (actually it was a firefish) heard
Octavia and swam over to stop the racket so he could go back
to sleep. That's all he did since there are not an awful lot of
fires under the sea. When he saw the problem, he mowed the
weeds off with his lawn mower. Octavia was free!

Then the fireman told Octavia, "I've seen bread commer-
cials on TV. Bread is something you put inside of you, not
outside."

"Mercy me," said Octavia. "Then if Jesus is the Bread of Life,
I need to get Him inside me. How can I do that?"

"Just ask Him to come into your heart," said the fireman.

So Octavia took off the wrappers and prayed, "Dear Jesus, I
give my heart to You." And her religion no longer was just
wrappings and carrying a song book. Now the happy song was
in her heart.

All Lessons

Begin the story by saying, "Either our faith can be a burden
or wings that lift us up."

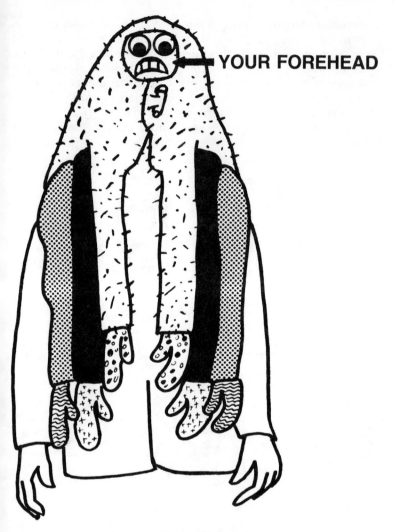

YOUR FOREHEAD

Figure 1 **Easy Object Lesson**

Easy Object Lesson

Show a burden by putting a rolled-up blanket on the back of your bowed neck. Show wings by folding the blanket to

convenient length, putting it behind your back, holding a corner in each hand, and flapping it like wings. Or put two bright sweaters around your shoulders and one over your head, pinned shut as shown in figure 1. Pin mittens or gloves to the sweater arms in advance. In front of the audience, stick on 1-1/2″ wiggle eyes and a down-turned paper mouth onto your forehead. Lean forward so the sweater arms sway. After Octavia accepts Jesus, turn the sad mouth upside down into a smile.

Figure 2 **Chalk Talk**

Puppet Talk

Put a huge book (the burden) on a puppet. Later pin wings, cut from a file folder, on the puppet.

Chalk Talk

See figure 2. Draw the bottle and say, "Octavia's religion was a burden, like medicine" (A). Turn the bottle into a sad man and say, "Such religion is sad" (B). Draw the wings and cover the frown with a smile (C).

29
Sticky Ricky

Stand firm. Let nothing move you. (1 Cor. 15:58)

"I want to be a hero for Jesus," said Ricky to himself.

"Then you have to be a hero today," said his wall calendar.

"You didn't say that," said Ricky. "Calendars can't talk."

"Never mind," said the calendar. "Tomorrow never comes. Be a hero today."

Then a roll of sticky tape said, "And whatever you do, you have to stick to it. The secret of success is being a sticker."

"Okay," said Ricky, "I'll stick to Bible reading."

No sooner did he get his Bible out, than Sissy said, "Hey, there's a good cartoon on TV. Read your Bible later."

"No, I have to stick to it, no matter what. I have to be a sticker," said Ricky. So he pulled a dirty gym sock over his head and hid in a pile of dirty clothes so Sissy couldn't tempt him.

Next, Ricky's brother said, "Let's play catch."

"No! I have to be a sticker! A sticker! A sticker!" said Ricky. He stuck a bag of ice cubes on his head until it turned green and pimply like a cucumber and hid in a bushel basket of cucumbers and kept on reading his Bible.

After he finished, he put a blue ribbon on himself, because for that day he was a hero for Jesus. He was a sticker, the secret of success.

Easy Object Lesson

See figure 1. Make a scotch tape boy from strips of masking tape, drawing the head or cutting it from a magazine or catalog (A). Wrap him around a glass, to carry him to your audience. Stick him to a book labeled "Bible" or to a Bible. With

each temptation, pretend to tug him from the Bible. Finally, stick a blue ribbon (B) on him. You may want to "try" to pry Ricky off with a hammer and a crowbar (or pretend to hammer a screwdriver point under Ricky and use the screwdriver like a crowbar). Grunt, groan, and pretend to wipe perspiration from your brow.

Puppet Talk

Prepare one side of a Bible with scotch tape loops. Stick the puppet to the Bible and try to pry him loose (see easy object lesson).

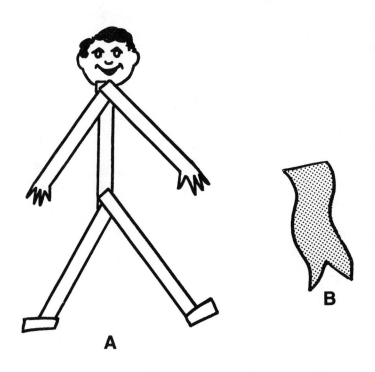

Figure 1 **Easy Object Lesson**

Chalk Talk

See figure 2. Draw the hero's reward, the loving cup (A) and turn it into Ricky (B).

Figure 2 **Chalk Talk**

30
Acting like Jesus

Let your light shine before men, that they may see your good deeds and praise your Father in heaven. (Matt. 5:16)

I hate myself, thought Topsy Turtle. When someone thinks like that she always fails, so Topsy would always strike out in baseball, trip over her own legs, and act clumsy. She was so shy she had no friends. Do you know anyone like that? She hated school so much that she got headaches every morning and begged, "Aw, Mom, do I have to go to school today?"

The other kids were mean and made fun of Topsy. She pretended not to care, but inside she hurt. She would crawl into her shell and cry. During school lunch, she cried so much that she had to eat the same bowl of soup three times. Her shell filled up with tears, so sleeping was like being on a waterbed. She was terribly seasick.

Then one day Jesus came to Topsy's school and became her friend. He encouraged her. When she caught a ball, He said, "Great! See, you can do it!" He was so kind. Pretty soon she loved school and was happy.

Actually, this Jesus was really just someone who acted like Him. Wouldn't it be wonderful if someone like that went to your school? Someone here could be like that. Want to know who? Open this door and see. [See object lessons.]

Easy Object Lesson

Hold a picture of Jesus or a sign saying "Jesus" over a child's face and say, "Wouldn't it be wonderful if people saw Jesus in you?"

Fun Object Lesson

See figure 1. Make a turtle by taping an oval piece of card-board to the back of your hand so the front of the rim comes up to the first knuckle of your middle finger. On this finger, tape a smaller cardboard oval for the turtle's head. Stick 1-1/8″ wiggle eyes to the head. Hang this hand straight down when showing the turtle. Wiggle your fingers to make a lively turtle. When you close your fist, the turtle's head and legs go into the shell. Omit the turtle's tail.

An alternative idea is to wear a big mirror under your jacket supported by a string around your neck. Pin a C-shaped door handle to your coat. Have the children use this handle to open the "door" (your coat) and see who could be like Jesus.

Puppet Talk

Follow the instructions for the fun object lesson, using a turtle puppet (see p. 94).

Figure 1 **Fun Object Lesson**

Chalk Talk

See figure 2. In telling the story say, "People saw Jesus in this person."

Figure 2 **Chalk Talk**

Thirty-five Object Lesson Ideas

1. Pull a puppet's skirt over its head and say, "A person wrapped up in himself makes a small package."
2. Wind up alarm clock: (a) "Without prayer we run down spiritually." (b) "We need prayer to awaken us to spiritual needs." (c) "A clock thought about having to tick twice a second, 120 times a minute, 63,072,000 times a year, and gave up until it remembered it only had to make one tick at a time." (Do tough jobs one step at a time.)
3. Unplug a light and say, "Apart from me you can do nothing" (John 15:5).
4. Show a paint can or brush and say, "Leaning against a newly painted fence will spoil your clothes and the paint job—you hurt yourself by hurting others."
5. Use a ball to demonstrate "bouncing back from defeat."
6. Flashlight: (a) Shine a flashlight under a puppet's skirt or through a paper person to demonstrate Matthew 5:16: "Let your light shine. . . ." (b) "We need to recharge spiritually through prayer."
7. Show a giant paper hand labeled "GOD" and a paper shield labeled "HUMANS." Say, "Human security fails [crumple the shield], but 'the eternal God is your refuge and underneath are the everlasting arms.' " (Deut. 33:27).
8. Display a bird nest, bird, or paper cutout of an egg. Say, "It's all right if birds fly over your head, but don't let them build a nest in your hair—that is, don't harbor bad thoughts."
9. Boat picture: (a) "An idle motor lets a boat drift downstream—we must grow for Christ or lose ground." (b) "It's not the gale but the set of the sail that determines our destination" (perseverance).
10. Show a string on a stick and say, "Be fishers of men."
11. Hold up a briefcase with "M.D." on it and say, "Christ heals sick souls."

12. Have a roll of paper stuck in your ear. Unroll the paper to show sins that keep us from hearing God's voice.
13. Display sachet (or perfume or a flower), a stone, a grater, and a match. Say, "When we come in contact with others, we can bless them with sweetness, be stoney, grate against them, or flare up in anger."
14. Presenting a drawer full of items, say, "We can't clean the drawer without removing the contents—we can't clean our hearts without asking God to remove our sins."
15. Play a tape recorder on a faster speed than the original recording. Say, "We must slow down and pray or life will be a spiritual jumble."
16. Show various bottles to demonstrate that the same Holy Spirit takes different forms in different people.
17. Hold up a checkbook and say, "Just as an overdrawn account makes checks worthless, spiritual power must be renewed."
18. Use crayons to show that the same picture looks different according to whether we use bright or dark colors. "Be joyful always" (1 Thess. 5:16).
19. Calendar: (a) Around each date, make a slit from which treasures can be removed to show that each day is the door of opportunity. (b) Throw calendar pages into a wastebasket to illustrate wasted chances to serve God or the value of accepting Christ while young.
20. Demonstrate with weeds that if you leave the condition of your soul to chance, "weeds" will take over.
21. Use cosmetics and soap to show that covering up sin won't get rid of it. God must cleanse us.
22. With a boomerang or mirror demonstrate that we reap what we sow (Gal. 6:7).
23. Use a saw and ax to tell the children that the steady Christian (saw) is better than the one who jumps in with mighty strokes, then tires out (ax).
24. With a candle and firecracker show that it is better to shine steadily for Jesus than to be a flash in the pan.
25. Hold up a lemon and say, "Squeezing doesn't make a lemon sour; it reveals inner sourness—troubles won't sour us if our hearts are sweet."
26. Put on and remove a mask, saying, "We can't hide our true nature from God."

27. Hold up an extension cord and say, "We must be channels of God's power to others."
28. Use a top or a bike to show that Christians must keep moving for God or fall down.
29. Display a shoe and say: (a) "Others follow our footsteps." (b) "A journey of a thousand miles begins with a single step." (c) "Don't judge until you walk in the other person's shoes."
30. Present a scrapbook and tell the children, "Our minds are scrapbooks of the good or bad we put into them."
31. Hold up an unfinished model plane or car and say, "It's sad to be a quitter."
32. Hold a file card, cut in the shape of a barred window, in front of your tongue as though your tongue were a beast that should be caged (James 3:7-8).
33. Display a kite and say, "A kite won't fly without a tail" (discipline).
34. Loaf of bread: (a) Crush a puppet under a loaf of bread to show that "man does not live on bread [material things] alone, but on every word that comes from the mouth of God" (Matt. 4:4). Then show the puppet soaring on a Bible equipped with paper wings to depict the life of one who lives by God's Word. (b) Use an empty bread wrapper to imprison a puppet to demonstrate that living for bread (material things) alone is either empty or a prison.
35. With a radio show there is always static (things that bother us), but if the music of love is stronger it will come out on top.

Children's Sermon Techniques

Animated Objects and Gimmicks

Personalize any object shown by adding eyes, a nose, and a mouth. Wiggle eyes and fake fur add flair. Stick eyes and other parts on with masking tape looped sticky side out.

Recommended wiggle eye sizes: fish and turtle novelty quickie puppets—1-1/2"; fist puppet—1-3/8"; goat novelty quickie puppet—1-1/8".

You may give your talk in answer to a phoney phoned question. Say, "There goes my phone," and make your sleeves into a phone, holding one sleeve to your mouth, the other to your ear. Say, "Hello," listen a bit and repeat what you "heard" (e.g., "You say that you want to know how to pray?"). Similarly, you may open a letter and answer it.

Bag Stage

Use a grocery bag as a stage, sticking the puppet up through a hole near the bag's bottom (figure 1).

Puppet Speech

A puppet's questions can advance a story. A shy puppet could whisper in your ear as you repeat its words. Or, when

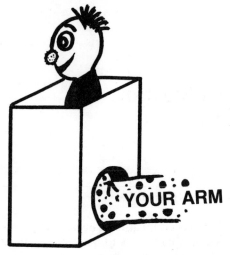

Figure 1 **Bag Stage**

Your free arm (not shown) supports the bag.

Figure 2 **Fist Puppet**

Tuck each end of a strip of fake fur into your fist for hair. Use a fist puppet with or without a bag stage.

90

the puppet speaks, hide your mouth behind a bag stage, Bible, hymnal, or file folder, with its top resting on your nose. The puppet can nod "yes" or shake its head "no." Sneezing and explosive humming sounds (laugh, cough, and cry) are easy as you can make them with your mouth shut.

Add to the illusion that the puppet is speaking by focusing your eyes on it, moving its head and body as well as its mouth. Disguise your voice by changing pitch, tonal quality, inflection, speaking rate, or by using accents. Open the puppet's mouth on every syllable it says, or nod its head if its mouth won't move.

The ventriloquial voice is a high nasal tone, muffled by tightening your throat muscles while breathing from the diaphram. Talk without moving your jaw or your lips. Substitute F or T for P, V or D for B, and NG for M while slurring over these substitute sounds, or else use dialogue that avoids P, B, and M. With practice you may learn to make these sounds with your tongue.

Easy Puppets

Fist puppet: Stick facial features to the back of your fist and wrap fake fur around your knuckles (figure 2). Wear a loose sleeve (the puppet's body) so the puppet's head can move in relation to it. For an alternative body, pin a bandana around your wrist.

Make this puppet into many animals by changing head features. Half raised fingers make cat ears (figure 3). Fully raised fingers make rabbit ears. Or use paper ears. Pin a dust mop over the cat's head to make a lion.

Figure 3   **Fist Cat Puppet**

To make a fist puppet with a moving mouth (figure 4), stick 1-1/2″ wiggle eyes and a 2″ pink pompon nose on your fingers. The eyes and nose must be big enough to cover the spaces between your fingers. Use masking tape loops on the first joints of your fingers to hold the fake fur hair, grain pointing forward. Open and shut your fingers to work the mouth. On your thumb stick a paper loop, just big enough for your closed fingers to cover. The bottom and sides of the loop are red lips with white teeth and a black center. For a lasting puppet, glue the features to a tan sock on your hand.

To make a spider (figure 5), stuff one glove into another one with its cuff turned in. Add wiggle eyes.

To make an octopus (figure 6), tape wiggle eyes and flesh colored paper strips to your hand.

Figure 4 **Fist Puppet with Moving Mouth**

Figure 5 **Spider**

Figure 6 **Octopus Puppet**

Novelty quickie puppets: Assemble the fish and goat puppets as shown in figure 7 in front of your audience. The fin and horn have handles held in your fist. Note the different finger and eye positions of the two animals. Wiggle your thumb to make these puppets talk.

To make a turtle puppet as shown in figure 8, tape an eye to your fist. To your arm, tape a pie tin or paper plate, with paper legs prestuck to it.

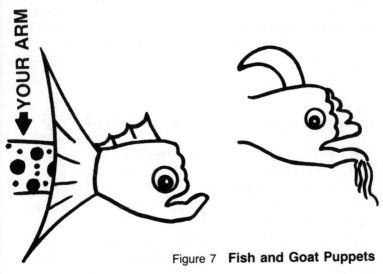

Figure 7 **Fish and Goat Puppets**

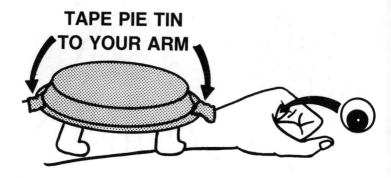

TAPE PIE TIN TO YOUR ARM

Figure 8 **Turtle Puppet**

Envelope puppets: (See figure 9). Fold in the bottom of a small envelope so the corners (X, X) meet together as lips (A-C). Add wiggle eyes, a pompon nose, and fake fur hair (D). For the body wrap a bandana around your wrist with a corner tucked in (E). Put masking tape tabs (F) inside the upper and lower jaws for your fingers to grab (use your thumb and ring finger in the lower jaw and your index and middle finger in the upper jaw). *Optional:* Color the envelope flesh color, the inner mouth black, and the lips red.

Tape a paper towel, or crepe paper (dotted areas in G-K) to the envelope to make another type of body. A paper fringe makes either centipede legs (G) or porcupine quills. Other body parts make a bird (H), frog (I), fish (J), mouse (K), or most any animal.

Glove Puppet Stunts for Amusing Children

Lay a paper on a table, then (unknown to you) have the puppet knock it off.

Look perplexed and replace the paper. Do repeatedly.

Repeatedly have the puppet close a hymnal in your hands and finally knock it to the floor.

Appear with a puppet hidden in a bag stage and say, "You don't know what's in this bag." Then (unknown to you) the

94

Figure 9 **Envelope Puppets**

95

puppet pops up and the children guess correctly. Whenever you look toward the bag, you barely miss seeing the puppet pop down. Repeat. Act outraged at the children's "lucky" guess. "How did you know that? Well, you don't know its name." When you ask the children if the puppet is named several names, it pops up and shakes its head no. At the mention of another name it nods yes. So the children say yes to your question this time. Again act outraged at their guessing. Use the same procedure to guess its age.

The puppet pops up and tickles your ear. You swat at your ear, remaking about how bad the flies are. Repeat. Next, the puppet bites your ear and you yell. Repeat. Then the puppet bites and twists and gnaws on your ear and you reach up and catch it in the act.

The puppet pulls off your snap-on tie (or scarf) and keeps eluding your free hand snatching for the tie. Then the puppet hits you on the face with the tie. Next the puppet pulls a small section of your shirt out from under your belt. In great embarrassment, you quickly tuck your shirt in. Repeat. Finally the puppet pulls out your shirt all the way across the front of your stomach, and you act mortified.

Give a talk against littering, picking up wads of paper previously scattered on the platform. Each time you put a wad in the stage bag the puppet secretly and immediately throws it out. Sometimes he hits you in the head with the wad, and you say, "Who hit me with that wad?" (Pretend you don't know the puppet is in the bag.) Finally, mention how much better the stage looks after you cleaned it, while the puppet dumps a huge amount of wads (preloaded) from the bag.